George Washington Carver

History Maker Bios

Matt Doeden

BARNES & NOBLE

NEW YORK

Illustrations by Tad Butler

Barnes & Noble, Inc.
122 Fifth Avenue
New York, NY 10011

ISBN-13: 978-0-7607-8960-5
ISBN-10: 0-7607-8960-6

Printed and bound in the United States of America

1 3 5 7 9 10 8 6 4 2

TABLE OF CONTENTS

INTRODUCTION

George Washington Carver was born a slave. He worked hard through poverty and racism to get an education. Then he used what he learned to help others. Over time, he became a true American success.

George was a scientist, a farmer, a teacher, and an artist. He had a talent for growing plants. His ideas greatly improved farming in the southern United States. George never sought fame or fortune. But he became well known for his discoveries.

This is his story.

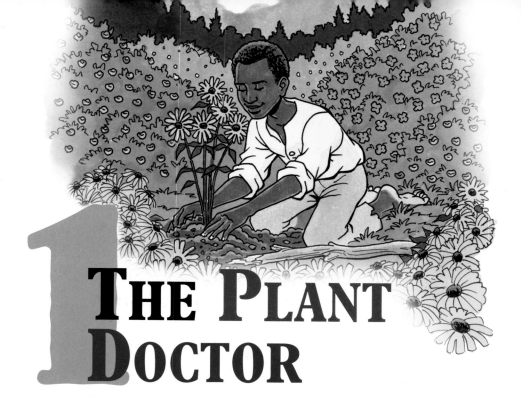

1 THE PLANT DOCTOR

George Washington Carver had a tough start in life. He was born around 1864 in Marion Township, Missouri. His mother was a slave named Mary. George's father was a slave at a nearby farm. He died in an accident two weeks after George's birth.

George and his mother had no last name. Most slaves didn't have a last name of their own. So they went by their first names only.

In early 1865, some men sneaked onto the farm of Moses and Susan Carver, George's owners. The men kidnapped Mary, George, and his sister. They took the slaves to sell them to other slave owners.

Moses and Susan cared about their slaves. They treated them almost like family. So they hired a neighbor named John Bentley to find Mary and the children. Within a few days, John found baby George. He had been left behind. He had a terrible cough and was near death. But John found no trace of the others.

George drew this picture of his birthplace.

Moses Carver (LEFT) was a German American. He raised George and Jim as his own sons.

Susan nursed George back to health. She and Moses agreed to raise George and his older brother, Jim. At that time, the Northern and Southern states were fighting the U.S. Civil War. The two sides disagreed about many issues, including whether slavery should be allowed in the United States. The North won the war in 1865. That same year, slavery ended in the Southern states. George and Jim were free. But they were part of the Carver family. So they stayed with Moses and Susan.

George's illness had left him weak. He couldn't do hard farmwork. So Susan taught him how to help around the house. He learned to cook, sew, and wash clothes. And best of all, Susan taught him to read. Most children who had been slaves could not read. They were not allowed to go to schools for white children.

George spent his time walking through the woods near his home. Plants fascinated him. So George started a garden. He kept it a secret because many people thought growing flowers was foolish.

George learned a lot about plants in the woods.

REMEMBERING CHILDHOOD

Later in life, George wrote about his childhood: "Day after day I spent in the woods alone in order to collect my floral beauties. . . . All sorts of vegetation seemed to thrive under my touch. . . . "

George took good care of his garden. He learned about soil and seeds. He also studied insects. He learned how they helped or harmed plants. "I wanted to know every strange stone, flower, insect, bird, or beast," George later said. Soon he knew more about how to grow healthy plants than most farmers did. George's neighbors went to him with questions. They even started calling him the plant doctor.

When the Carvers' best apple tree started to die, George had a solution. He climbed the tree and found a branch that insects had been eating.

George told Moses to cut off the branch. His solution worked. The tree became healthy again.

When George was eleven, he learned of a school that taught black students. He badly wanted to attend. But the school was eight miles away in the town of Neosho. He had no way to get back and forth.

Nothing was more important to young George than attending school. So he told the Carvers that he was leaving for Neosho. Moses and Susan didn't stand in his way.

George used this slate at school in Neosho.

One morning, George set out for Neosho with just a little food and a few small belongings. George walked the eight miles to the schoolhouse. But when he got there, he found that it had closed for the evening.

George needed somewhere to spend the night. He found a nearby barn. He climbed onto a pile of hay and went to sleep. The barn's owners, Mariah and Andrew Watkins, discovered George the next morning.

George did chores for Andrew (LEFT) and Mariah Watkins. The Watkinses let him stay with them while he went to school in Neosho.

George's brother, Jim (RIGHT), came to live with the Watkinses too.

The Watkinses were an African American couple. George's desire to go to school impressed them. They invited him to stay with them. He repaid them by helping with household chores.

George introduced himself to Mariah as "Carver's George." He still had no last name. Mariah was shocked. She told George that he needed a proper last name. From that moment on, he would be George Carver.

George had a new name, a new home, and a place to learn. In time, his brother, Jim, even joined him in Neosho. Life was good.

2 QUEST FOR KNOWLEDGE

Geroge lived with Mariah and Andrew for three years. He learned all he could in school. But by the time he was about thirteen, he felt that his teachers in Neosho had nothing more to teach him. He loved the Watkinses, but it was time to move on. So George headed to Fort Scott, Kansas. Fort Scott was a larger town with several schools. George hoped to learn more there.

Life in Fort Scott was tough. George was truly on his own. He was hungry and poor. He worked at whatever job he could get. He attended school when he had enough time left over. At night, he studied by candlelight. Some of the white students picked on him. But George was learning. That was enough for him.

Meanwhile, George had a new passion. He had seen a painting of flowers at one of his jobs. He decided that he wanted to be an artist. He spent his free time drawing. With his art, his jobs, and his schooling, he was a very busy young man.

George was about 13 when he moved to Fort Scott.

In the 1800s, horses provided transportation in Fort Scott, Kansas.

In 1879, when George was about fifteen, he saw something that affected him deeply. A mob of white people dragged a black man out of the Fort Scott jail. The man had been accused of a crime but had not yet gone to trial. The mob beat him, poured heating oil on him, and set him on fire. Violent acts such as this were called lynchings. Lynchings were common at the time, especially in the South. Many blacks accused of crimes were never given fair trials. White citizens often took the law into their own hands.

The lynching convinced George that it was time to get out of Fort Scott. He packed his things that very night and set off again. For the next several years, George moved from town to town. He searched for work and went to school when he had enough time and money.

Around this time, George began using the middle initial *W*. He once had a classmate also named George Carver and had wanted to set himself apart. At some point, the *W* became "Washington."

George's first schools had only black students.

In 1885, George Washington Carver finally graduated from high school in Minneapolis, Kansas. George still loved to learn. He knew what he wanted to do next—go to college. So he sent an application to Highland College in Kansas. He was excited when the college accepted him.

George worked hard that summer to earn money for his schooling. He arrived at the Highland campus on September 20, 1885. But when he tried to sign up for classes, he was in for a shock.

About one thousand people lived in Minneapolis, Kansas, when George went to high school there.

Irvin Hall at Highland College was built in 1858. George applied to go to school at Highland in 1885. But the college did not admit black students.

The school's president told George that he couldn't attend. When Highland had accepted him, school officials had thought he was white. Highland refused to admit black students.

George was crushed. All he wanted to do was learn. But he couldn't change the rules. Disappointed, he went to Ness County, Kansas. He took up farming there. He raised crops and did experiments with plants. He also continued to work on drawings and paintings.

Over the next four years, George saved up enough money to try another college. He traveled to Simpson College in Indianola, Iowa. This time, he was allowed to enroll. At the age of twenty-five, George was finally a college student. He set up his own laundry business to help pay the bills.

George enjoyed all sorts of classes. At first, he wanted to study art. But he decided to focus on botany, the study of plants.

Open to All

Matthew Simpson founded Simpson College in 1860. Matthew was a bishop in the Methodist Church. He was also a friend of President Abraham Lincoln. Matthew believed in the equality of all men. At a time when many colleges refused to enroll black students, Simpson College welcomed George. But of the college's three hundred students, George was the only African American.

George stands beside one of his paintings.

George soon moved on to Iowa State College of Agriculture (the science of farming) and Mechanic Arts in Ames, Iowa. He worked as a custodian there to earn a living. At night, he studied by candlelight. In 1894, all of his hard work paid off. He earned a college degree. Graduating from college was quite an achievement for a former slave. But George wasn't done yet.

3 STUDENT AND TEACHER

George had impressed his professors at Iowa State. They told him to continue his studies to get a graduate degree. They even offered him a teaching job while he was a graduate student. George happily accepted it. He taught classes on agriculture and botany. He also took charge of the college's greenhouses, the school's special buildings for growing plants. In two years, he earned a master's degree in agriculture.

During George's years at Iowa State, he had started to make a name for himself. He had discovered a fungus that was harming local soybean crops and another that was hurting maple trees. He had also made fliers that told farmers how to fight crop diseases. Fewer crop diseases meant more healthy crops for farmers to sell.

In classes at Iowa State, George (BACK ROW, SECOND FROM RIGHT) was the only African American student.

Booker T. Washington was born in 1856. He had been a slave too.

In May 1896, George's life changed forever. Booker T. Washington had written him a letter. Booker had started a school in Tuskegee, Alabama. Booker wanted to teach black students the skills they needed to succeed. He asked for George to help him by directing the school's agriculture department.

"I cannot offer you money . . . or fame," Booker wrote. "I offer you in their place work—hard, hard work."

George didn't waste time in deciding. He packed his things and headed south to Alabama. But when he arrived at Tuskegee Normal and Industrial Institute, he was shocked. At Iowa State, he'd had a good science lab. He'd had proper scientific tools. At Tuskegee, he had none of that. He was starting over with almost nothing.

George had his new students help him get equipment for the lab. They collected jars, bottles, and pots and pans. They could use those tools to do basic experiments with soil and plants. George and his students didn't have much. But they made the best of what they found.

Students helped George get these jars, lamps, and bottles for his lab at Tuskegee.

Teaching wasn't George's only job at Tuskegee. He also did research. His first big project was important. In 1897, farmers in the region were struggling. George wanted to find a way to help them.

Cotton was the most important crop in the South at the time. But Alabama's soil wasn't producing good cotton crops. George knew why. Cotton plants are hard on the soil. They suck up all the nutrients, the substances in food that keep animals and plants healthy. After a few seasons, the soil can't give the plants what they need to live and grow.

Research was part of George's job at Tuskegee.

Cotton is a soft, white material that grows around the seeds of a cotton plant.

George tested an idea called crop rotation. Crop rotation is the practice of planting different crops each year on the same patch of land. George told farmers to plant peas and sweet potatoes instead of cotton. Those crops would let the soil build up nutrients.

Farmers didn't like the idea. They couldn't make much money with peas and sweet potatoes. But George showed them new uses for the crops. He also explained that growing them would improve the soil. After a year or two, the soil would be ready to grow cotton again. A good cotton crop would bring in the money the farmers needed.

Many farmers followed George's advice. They grew other crops. Finally, it was time to plant cotton again. Farmers looked forward to the payoff George had promised—healthy cotton crops.

At first, the plan worked perfectly. The cotton plants grew well. People expected a great harvest. But then disaster struck. Small insects called boll weevils got into the cotton plants. The insects destroyed the crop.

BOLL WEEVIL

The boll weevil is a small beetle. It feeds on cotton plants. Adult boll weevils lay their eggs inside cotton plants. The young that hatch look like tiny worms. They quickly destroy the cotton. The insects take just a few weeks to grow from eggs into adults. This short life cycle allows the pests to multiply and spread rapidly.

An adult boll weevil

The farmers didn't know what to do. All their hard work was ruined. They looked to George for answers. He told them to plow under their cotton and plant peanuts instead. Many laughed at him. Peanuts weren't used for much at the time. Some farmers didn't think they would be able to sell enough peanuts to make a living. But other farmers listened to George. They followed his advice and planted peanuts. George had work to do. He needed to find ways to use all the peanuts they would have.

4 THE AMAZING PEANUT

round 1910, George entered his laboratory with a purpose. He knew that peanuts were a healthy food. But that wasn't enough reason for people to buy lots of them. If farmers were going to make money growing peanuts, George needed to find new uses for the crop.

Peanuts are filled with nutrients. They contain proteins, oils, starches, and more. George did experiments with these substances. Soon he was finding many new uses for the peanut. He learned to use peanuts to make cooking oil, milk, cheese, peanut butter, and other products. He even created drinks, lotions, soaps, and medicines from the substances in peanuts.

George experiments with peanuts.

George wanted to introduce his discoveries in an exciting way. So he invited businesspeople from the area to lunch at the college. He fed them a big meal with soup, a main course that tasted like chicken, and even cookies and ice cream for dessert. After everyone had finished, George announced that everything they'd eaten had been made with peanuts.

As word of George's discoveries spread, the demand for peanuts grew in the United States. Farmers could sell enough peanuts to earn a living. George had done what he'd set out to do.

A woman stands in a peanut field. A stack of harvested peanuts is behind her.

George (FAR RIGHT) teaches a class at Tuskegee.

George continued to teach and do research at Tuskegee. Through the years, he made a name for himself among farmers and scientists. In 1920, a peanut-growers' group asked George to speak in Montgomery, Alabama. He arrived at Montgomery City Hall in his suit, ready for the meeting. But a sign above the door read No Coloreds. African Americans weren't allowed in the building. George sent the doorman inside to tell the group that he had arrived. He waited patiently until the doorman let him in to speak to the group. Despite his growing fame, George still struggled against racism in his everyday life.

Chinese farmers raised peanuts too. In 1920, they started to sell their peanuts in the United States.

The demand for peanuts had changed again by that year. China had noticed that peanuts sold well in the United States. Many farmers in China started selling their peanuts to U.S. buyers. Chinese farmers didn't charge much for their peanuts. But U.S. farmers couldn't afford to charge so little. Buyers were looking for the lowest prices. So they bought the cheaper peanuts from Chinese farmers. Soon U.S. peanut farmers weren't making any money.

U.S. peanut growers wanted help from the government. They wanted Congress to place a tariff on peanuts. A tariff is a tax on goods that come from outside the country. Placing a tariff on peanuts would raise the price of peanuts from China. If peanuts from China were more expensive, then people would buy U.S. peanuts again.

Congress decided to hold a meeting about tariffs. Peanut farmers wanted George to attend the meeting and speak for them. On January 20, 1921, George stood before a committee of the U.S. Congress. He had to convince the committee to place a tariff on peanuts. And he had only ten minutes to speak.

George spoke to a congressional committee in the Capitol.

George spoke with passion. He talked about the importance of peanuts to southern farmers. He told the committee about new uses for peanuts. The committee members were fascinated. After George's ten minutes were up, they begged him to continue.

GEORGE'S SUIT

George had little use for wealth. He almost always turned down pay raises. And George owned just one suit! When friends suggested that he buy a

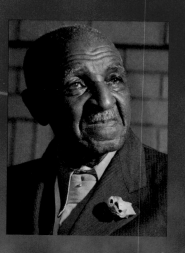

new one, he always declined. Every day, George put a fresh flower into a buttonhole on his suit. He had always loved flowers, and they were all the decoration he needed.

George kept going. He showed samples of many new products he had created. When his speech was done, everyone stood and clapped. George had convinced them. Congress placed a high tariff on peanuts. Once again, U.S. farmers could grow peanuts to make a living.

George's speech made national news. People were amazed that the former slave had done so much to help farmers. His story touched people around the nation. George Washington Carver was a true American success story.

5 THE HELPFUL EXPERT

George's fame grew. Farmers and businesspeople came to Tuskegee to get his advice. George was happy to help. He never charged anyone for his advice. He didn't try to make money on his inventions. Being rich didn't interest him. As long as he had his work and his paints, he was happy.

"The Lord charges me nothing for knowledge," he told people. "I will charge you the same."

Meanwhile, George kept up his research. He hadn't cracked all the peanut's secrets yet. He made many more discoveries. He learned that massages with peanut oil helped ease the pain of people crippled by a disease called polio. The peanut-oil massages weren't a cure. But they made patients' lives easier. (Scientists later found that it was the massages, not the peanut oil itself, that helped patients.)

PEANUTS EVERYWHERE

George came up with hundreds of uses for peanuts. Many helped create foods. But others used peanuts in entirely new ways. Below is a list of some of George's products made from peanuts.

beauty cream	paints
cloth dyes	paper
gasoline	plastic
ink	shampoo
instant coffee	soap

George never married. But he was always surrounded by people. Three U.S. presidents met with him: Theodore Roosevelt, Calvin Coolidge, and Franklin Delano Roosevelt. The prince of Sweden came to spend three weeks with George. Inventor Thomas Edison and automaker Henry Ford were George's friends. Henry was so impressed with George that he paid for a modern agriculture laboratory to be built at Tuskegee.

President Franklin D. Roosevelt (FRONT RIGHT) congratulates George on his work with peanuts.

Henry Ford (LEFT) and George were friends.

After World War II started in 1939, Henry asked George for advice. The nation was facing a rubber shortage. Rubber comes from a certain type of tree. It is used in car and airplane tires. Henry was looking for ways to make a new kind of rubber. George helped Henry to make synthetic, or man-made, rubber from sweet potatoes.

George also looked for ways to keep food from spoiling. He worked with chemicals that help prevent food from going bad. And he taught people how to dry or can food to eat later.

George's fame never changed him. "How far you go in life depends on your being tender with the young, compassionate with the aged . . . and tolerant of the weak and the strong," he said. "Because someday in life you will have been all of these."

George's help was always available to all people. He held visiting days at Tuskegee so that even poorer farmers with small farms could learn from him. He also started an Agricultural School on Wheels. The school was a truck that traveled to communities to deliver helpful farming information and to give demonstrations.

George's school truck was named after the founder of Tuskegee, Booker T. Washington.

In late 1942, seventy-nine-year-old George fell down a flight of stairs. He never recovered from the fall. He died on January 5, 1943. On his gravestone was a single sentence. It read: "He could have added fortune to [his] fame, but caring for neither, he found happiness and honor in being helpful to the world." It was a good description of George's life.

TIMELINE

In the year . . .

1865 slave raiders kidnapped George, his mother, and his sister.
John Bentley returned George to Moses and Susan Carver.
the North won the U.S. Civil War.
slavery ended in Missouri.

1875 George set off for Neosho, Missouri, so he could attend school there. `Age 11`

1877 he moved to Fort Scott, Kansas.

1879 he left Fort Scott after witnessing a lynching. `Age 15`

1885 he graduated from high school in Minneapolis, Kansas. `Age 21`
he was accepted to Highland College, but he wasn't allowed to enroll because he was black.

1890 he enrolled at Simpson College.

1894 he graduated from Iowa State and took a job as a teacher.

1896 he earned his master's degree. `Age 32`
Booker T. Washington offered him a teaching job at Tuskegee Institute.
George began teaching at Tuskegee.
he did research on peanuts and other crops.

1921 he convinced a congressional committee to place a tariff on peanuts. `Age 57`

1942 he worked with Henry Ford to develop a rubber made from sweet potatoes.

1943 he died on January 5. `Age 79`
President Franklin Roosevelt dedicated the George Washington Carver National Monument in Missouri.

REMEMBERING GEORGE

In July 1943, President Franklin Roosevelt dedicated the George Washington Carver National Monument near George's childhood home in Missouri. The monument includes a statue of George, a nature trail, and a museum. It was the first national monument dedicated to an African American.

Many other honors have come since George's death. He has been on two postage stamps. The *USS George Washington Carver*, a Navy submarine, was dedicated in 1966. And in 1990, George became part of the National Inventors Hall of Fame.

The memory of George Washington Carver lives on long after his death. He wanted to spend his life helping people, and that's exactly what he did.

The USS GEORGE WASHINGTON CARVER.

FURTHER READING

Adair, Gene. *George Washington Carver, Botanist.* New York: Chelsea House, 1989.
This biography profiles the life, education, and accomplishments of George Washington Carver.

Gardner, Robert. *Science Projects about Plants.* Springfield, NJ: Enslow Publishers, 1999.
This title guides young botanists through more than thirty experiments involving plants.

Hall, Margaret. *Peanuts.* Chicago: Heinemann Library, 2003.
Discusses the history, uses, and life cycle of the peanut. Hall also explains how farmers grow and harvest peanut crops.

Sullivan, Otha Richard. *African American Inventors.* New York: Wiley, 1998.
Profiles the lives and discoveries of twenty-five African American inventors. Featured inventors include George Washington Carver and Benjamin Banneker.

WEBSITES

George Washington Carver National Monument
http://www.nps.gov/archive/gwca/expanded/gwc.htm
This National Park Service site includes information about George Washington Carver's life and research, as well as photos, quotations, and park information.

National Inventors Hall of Fame—Inventor Profile
http://www.invent.org/hall_of_fame/30.html This page, created by the National Inventors Hall of Fame, describes Carver's important discoveries.

Tuskegee University
http://www.tuskegee.edu The home page for Tuskegee University includes the early history of the school as Tuskegee Normal and Industrial Institute for Negroes.

SELECT BIBLIOGRAPHY

Burchard, Peter Duncan. "George Washington Carver: For His Time and Ours."http://www.nps.gov/applications/ parks/gwca/ppdocuments/Special%20History%20Study .pdf. 2005. (December 18, 2006).

Coil, Suzanne M. *George Washington Carver*. New York: Franklin Watts, 1990.

Elliott, Lawrence. *George Washington Carver: The Man Who Overcame*. Englewood Cliffs, NJ: Prentice Hall, 1966.

Holt, Rackham. *George Washington Carver: An American Biography*. Garden City, NY: Doubleday, Doran, 1943.

Hunter J. H. *Saint, Seer and Scientist: The Remarkable Story of George Washington Carver of Tuskegee, Alabama.* Toronto: Evangelical Publishers, 1939.

Imes, G. Lake. *I Knew Carver*. Harrisburg, PA: J. Horace McFarland, 1943.

McMurry, Linda. *George Washington Carver: Scientist and Symbol*. Oxford: Oxford University Press, 1981.

Sullivan, Otha Richard. *African American Inventors*. New York: Wiley, 1998.

INDEX

Acknowledgments

For photographs and artwork: The images in this book are used with the permission of: Library of Congress, pp. 4 (LC-J601-302), 17 (LC-USZ62-117666), 19 (HABS KANS,22-HILA,1-1), 24 (LC-USZ62-49568), 35 (LC-USZ62-116673), 36 (LC-USW38-000165-D); George Washington Carver National Monument, pp. 7, 8, 9, 12, 13, 15, 21; Courtesy National Park Service, Museum Management Program and Tuskegee Institute National Historic Site, Slate, H 16.4,W 21, D 1.2 cm, http://www.cr.nps.gov/museum/exhibits/tuskegee/1gimage/gwc9.htm, p. 11; © CORBIS, p. 16; Kansas State Historical Society, p. 18; Iowa State University Library/Special Collections Department, p. 23; © Bettmann/CORBIS, p. 25; © MPI/Hulton Archive/Getty Images, p. 26; National Cotton Council, p. 27; © George D. Lepp/CORBIS, p. 29; Tuskegee University, pp. 31, 33; © Brown Brothers, pp. 32, 40; © Hulton Archive/Getty Images, p. 34; From the Collections of Henry Ford Museum and Greenfield Village (P.O.930), p. 41; National Archives, p. 42 (16-G-280-S-2544C); © SuperStock, Inc./SuperStock, p. 45.

Front cover: Courtesy of the Simpson College Archives
Back cover: USDA Photo

For quoted material: p. 10 (top), Letter from George Washington Carver to Mss. Liston and Budd, 1897?, Tuskegee Institute Archives, 1, 2, quoted in Peter Duncan Burchard, *George Washington Carver: For His Time and Ours,* National Parks Service, 2005, http://www.nps.gov/applications/parks/gwca/ppdocuments/Special%20History%20Study.pdf (December 18, 2006); p. 10 (bottom), "Tuskegee Institute," National Park Service, 2006, http://www.nps.gov/archive/bowa/tuskin.html (December 18, 2006); p. 24, 38, Suzanne M. Coil, *George Washington Carver* (New York: Franklin Watts, 1990); p. 42, Otha Richard Sullivan, *African American Inventors* (New York: Wiley, 1998).